Bug

JOKES

A Buddy Book
by **Hugh Moore**

Buddy BOOKS

More Jokes!

VISIT US AT

www.abdopub.com

Published by ABDO Publishing Company, 4940 Viking Drive, Suite 622, Edina, Minnesota 55435.
Copyright © 2005 by Abdo Consulting Group, Inc. International copyrights reserved in all countries. No
part of this book may be reproduced in any form without written permission from the publisher.

Printed in the United States.

Edited by: Sarah Tieck
Contributing Editors: Jeff Lorge, Michael P. Goecke
Graphic Design: Deborah Coldiron
Illustrations by: Deborah Coldiron and Maria Hosley

Library of Congress Cataloging-in-Publication Data

Moore, Hugh, 1970-
   Bug jokes / Hugh Moore.
      p. cm. — (More jokes!)
   Includes index.
   ISBN 1-59197-870-X
      1. Insects—Juvenile humor. 2. Riddles, Juvenile. I. Title. II. Series.

PN6231.I56M55 2005
818'.5402—dc22

                                              2004057515

What song do bees like to sing in stormy weather?

What do you call a mosquito when you cross it with a hippo?

4

I'm not sure, but if it stings you, you're in big trouble!

How does a flea get from place to place?

By itch-hiking!

What are the smartest insects?

Spelling bees!

What do you do with a sick wasp?

Take it to a wasp-ital!

What do you call little bugs that live on the moon?

Luna ticks!

Customer: Waiter, what is this bug doing in my alphabet soup?

Waiter: Learning to read!

What did one worm say to the other when he was late getting home?

Where in earth have you been?

Why was the glowworm unhappy?

Because her children weren't that bright!

What did the woodworm say to the chair?

It's been nice gnawing you!

Who can leap tall poodles in a single bound?

Why are spiders good baseball players?

Because they know how to catch flies!

What is a tick's favorite game?

Tick-tac-toe!

What is the best year for grasshoppers?

Leap year!

How does a spider greet a fly?

"I'm so pleased to eat you!"

What's spiral in shape and very crowded?

A snail with a houseguest!

Which mosquito attacked Dorothy and Toto?

The wicked itch of the west!

What did the flea say when the puppy ran away?

Dog-gone!

Which bee can't buzz?

The mumble bee!

What comes after a mayfly?

A June bug!

What do two termites say when they see a house on fire?

What is the slowest way to send a letter?

The U.S. snail!

Why did the bees go on strike?

For more honey and shorter flowers!

What do you get if you cross a centipede and a chicken?

Enough drumsticks to feed an army!

Why did the spider cross the information superhighway?

To get to her Web site!

What do you call it when a big computer bug has bitten you?

A megabyte!

Which arthropod has mastered the metric system?

The centipede!

Why did mama flea look so sad?

All her children were going to the dogs!

What kind of ant walks on two legs?

Your aunt!

What goes "Zzub, zzub, zzub"?

A bee flying backwards!

How do you swat flies in Texas?

With a tennis racket!

What do you call a mosquito with a tin suit?

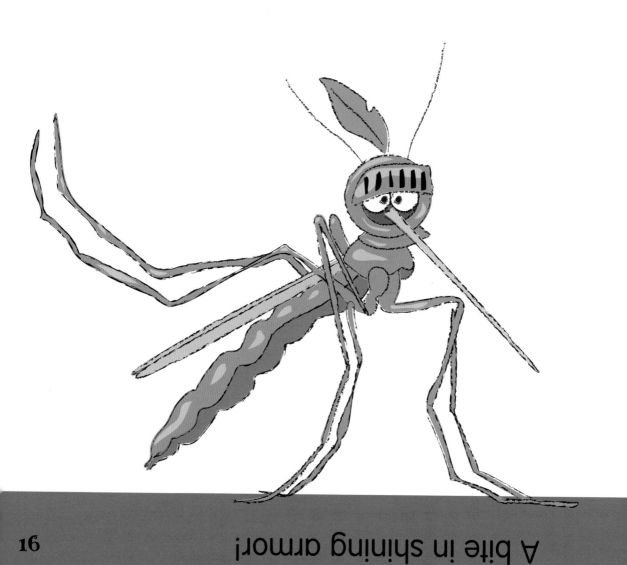

A bite in shining armor!

Where would you put an injured insect?

In an ant-bulance!

What is the insect's favorite game?

Cricket!

What did one girl firefly say to the other?

You glow girl!

What did the mosquito say the first time it saw a camel?

Did I do that?

What do you call a nervous insect?

A jitterbug!

Why did the worm decide to sleep late?

Because he didn't want the early bird to catch him!

Why was the inchworm angry?

He had to convert to the metric system!

Why do bees have sticky hair?

Because they have honeycombs!

What did the judge say when the
stinkbug walked into the courtroom?

How do you start a lightning
bug race?

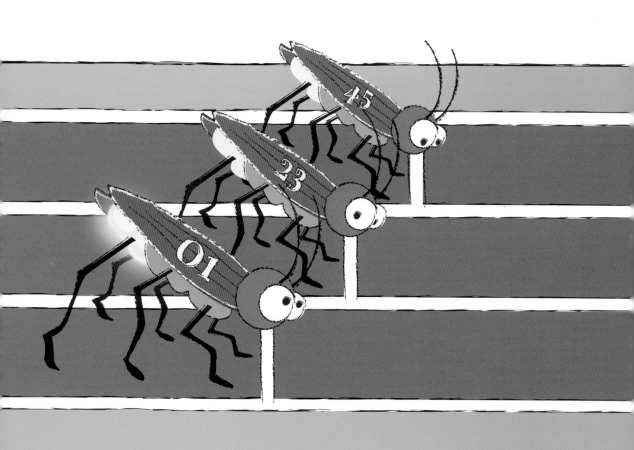

Say, "On your mark! Get set! Glow!"

What do you call a 100-year-old ant?

An ant-ique!

Why do bees hum?

Because they don't know the words!

How do we know bees watch TV?

They have antennae!

What did the male bee call his darling queen?

Honey!

What did one firefly say to the other?

Gotta glow now!

Why did the insect get kicked out of the park?

He was a litterbug!

What do bees chew?

Bumble-gum!

Why wouldn't they let the butterfly into the dance?

Because it was a moth-ball!

What do you call two spiders who just got married?

Web Sites

Visit ABDO Publishing Company on the World Wide Web. Joke Web sites for children are featured on our Book Links page. These links are monitored and updated to provide the silliest information available.

www.abdopub.com